By the same author

prose

Passing Duration
Writing Out of Character, with Rod Mengham and John Wilkinson
The Library of Label

translation

Rilke I IV VI, with Geoff Ward and Ian Patterson
Orpheus
Safety
VILLON by Jean Calais
After Lucretius

poetry

Left Under a Cloud
Mon Canard
Answer to Doctor Agathon
Erasers
Leaving
Emergency Measures
Oriflamme Day, with Benjamin Friedlander
Four Lectures
Plane Debris
The Bell Clerk's Tears Keep Flowing
One or Two Love Poems from the White World
Li(v)es of the Artist
The Knife

plays

A and C: an Idyll in One Act
Tennyson
Zuza Play
Nomad Life

essays

The Monkey's Donut

fiction

Château D'If

MON CANARD

SIX POEMS

Stephen Rodefer

THE FIGURES • 2000

Cover painting: *Flowers #9,* acrylic & collage on canvas, 60 x 60"
by Donald Baechler, 1997

A version of "Mon Canard" was published in Paris (O Pasternak) on New Year's Day, 1995, in an edition of 25, each with a hand-made cover by the author. Since then, portions of the poem have appeared in ANGEL EXHAUST and SNARE, enabled by Andrew Duncan and Drew Gardner. The poem grew from a translation of Annette Messager's "Les qualificatifs donnés aux femmes." The author is responsible for any additions, alterations or mistakes there-in.

"Daydreams of Frascati" (with drawings by Chip Sullivan) was published by Sake Forbear, "Erasers" saw print in the Equipage series. "Answer to Doctor Agathon" came out in *Cambridge Poetical Histories*. "Arabesque at Bar" appeared in *Parataxis*, and "Stewed and Fraught with Birds" was published in *Lingo 8: Pulp Poetry Supplement.* Thanks to Alastair Johnston, Rod Mengham, Peter Riley, Drew Milne, Irene Pasternak and Michael Gizzi for their reading, and to Reptilian Lettrist Graphics for page 114.

The Figures, 5 Castle Hill, Great Barrington MA 01230
Distributed by Small Press Distribution, Berkeley, CA
Available in the UK from Alfred David Editions
76 Rossiter Road, London, SW12 9RX

The publisher wishes to thank the Saul Rosen Foundation and Hand Hollow Foundation for their generous and continued support.

ISBN 1-930589-03-4

to the left, Katrine, and to the right, Dewey
—from Cambridge—
these few years

CONTENTS

DAYDREAMS OF FRASCATI

As our italicized romance crosses the bar again, we find our little contrivance being blinkered by Papal authority through a landscape of elegy and illusion. A microphone under each plant was a cardinal rule. Obsessions never become free until they enthrall you. Maybe a little weird scenario over on the side for the Marquis, where the chaste can be ravished if they like. No apples in the Apennines. Where the Appian wall alots its orgies to Fresca stands, we aright ourselves under corresponding skies. Thus . . .

Oh look—the ladder of the horizon in the lying tree. Not the directest way to the Pearly Gates, but it helps to upset the church mice and to spread out the sheets for our penultimate libation on these graven slopes.

Plastic Phoneme Man dives into the ground to be cleansed of his identity as a comet, counting on his ersatz knuckles for the cheeky husband. Imperfect cuckold. Come into the garden, you mouldy clerics, the black bat night is blown.

Your trail of sky has skewered my gyroscope so punctually, as true as cupid's arrower with his balmy glance at the department thing.

Dude x'd the public sculpture proposed by the art committee for the back yard. Better a pinhead or some mechanical anteater than a theory of asymmetry or the solace of good forms. The prize is a box of Macanudo Greens.

The poplars dissect the Etruscan chapparal, like olives of the bar computing the terraces for stool pigeons. In such a landscape, who can escape the assassination of the indoor. A villa in Avila would be more palatabler than a banquet of Borgias with ideas.

Just paint the junk Heraclitus cajoled the gods to cast down upon us, and call it garden fate. Hold a mirror up to the unnatural and leave it there, disguised as a façade or at least an earthwork. Where we were when we were you know where.

Oh, the little mouses, sniffing up the hill for a timely twitch and a smoke. Of course, Murillo himself would just lay back in his dare-you glory, like a brush with mushrooms—all poison, all delicious, all tinted pink.

I am come to be your cartop Ajax, waxing toward an invitation to an opening in some hedgerow. Our Leninist principles have toppled, to become fabulous and Sylvan once again. We are the last metaphysical activists in American nihilism. We demand a Pope from the Bronx.

Oh academy, oh gainsville, oh tenured night—how parallel is the cultivation of difference amidst the undifferentiated culture of the bigshots. You may now open my observatory again like a manhole, before some crazed double-breasted guy emerges from its cover in galoshes. The bush mills are staggered and my stasis is inscribed as a cloud.

Where do you want the beehive in your palm tree? May I draw the hip again, within yon hedge, of a bent comedienne by name of ball? Give me your leaves, your kerbs, your unwashed jeans. And get your luminous comments out of my hair, mon, I have to be peculiar now. It's hoops I'm into, and sideshows. Read letters in the sky.

Mira! Windows, envelopes, innuendoes. How the animals stray, rivetted in place. A site-specific site, like a grove of academics convening for some high-class chatter by a fount, which answers their questions by recycling water. I can see the Dome below – looks like nothing so much as a roof over a head. Must be the smoke of a papacy expiring on its own breath.

Let me juggle now a few of these inimitables, on which may sit the totality of your bottom line, spiked with nardy. Which I might eat, were I not absorbed by a theory of dirt or drought, confronting the historical beach in a scrape at Ocean View.

Come on down to this precipice a spell and lace the film with surge. Just over the hill may be the Capitol or the

Levant, to which the celebrants can be ferried willy nilly as they please. Recorders will be within the oars. And on the *other side*, I've got a couple of friends with vans.

Isn't it jarring how the sky above the colored gravel can't scratch the surface of the horizontal? Something about denim makes us languish to be there, half wishing we were French. It throws off the spectacle of preservation, and gets some plum to prove to be as human as an artifice.

The ditch that leads to the absent, leads also to some crank of pergola, over the hollow, resounding well. It pings to us from out the sibylline. For what? Burnt out and bought by the proud from nine to three. But after that, crowned with grapes for Aesculapius.

Christ, no tidbits please. A hunger for alternation explodes with your hammer and that sickle. Snore on, leviathan, across some boundless deep. Put a bowling ball in the Diorama, the last available in all of Indiana, just to amuse clairvoyant friends. Let them murder to dissect, we rake to replicate, we needle to amuse.

Oh good God, another cenotaph. Or do you prefer a crypt? Nice place for upright contact. Let us mount once more this sober request for spirits in some Grail legend Gayle would understand. The cypress trees erect their mystical choruses to get down, by rising up into a mythologic sky.

Fabulous wonder. A few years to the end of the mill and it's still pictures. Moving past the idea of the inside as the outside, the can opens on a dream of wacking startles. Not far from Civitavecchia, I imagine, where the slope butts the azure of the foam a little sordidly. But that was Rome. A place for undined lovers, awaiting the future's kiss.

ERASERS

I feel like burning texts for firewood. I feel like spreading ink on my toast and smearing the paper with butter.

Your sister by this time must have got the Devonshire ees *—short* ees*—you know 'em. They are the prettiest* ees *in the language.*

I take it upon myself to denounce intimacy. I have my nerves and my dizziness. I aspire to absolute rest and continuous daylight . . .to know nothing, to teach nothing, to will nothing, to want nothing—to sleep and still to sleep today is my only wish.

BEATING ERASERS

to H E & R

We banged
the two
together
at recess
and breathed
the chalky cloud
of several
wiped-out
number ones
no longer
on the boards
until they were
black again
with their
white felt stripes.
It's amazing
how indentation
makes an echo,
how space
looks blank
and returns to class.
What person

deserves
another's love?
What
person
does not?

There are women of great experience
who lying with a man
elevate their feet vertically
in the air and put
lamps on them
full of oil
with wicks burning.
While the night suffuses
them they keep the lamps
steady and burning
and the oil is not spilled.
Their commingling is in no way
impeded by this display
although great practice is demanded
on both their parts.

I saw the mud today.
She was amiable,
but breathed behind
a veil of judges
none representable.
The addition
of the C is really sub-
traction. Amicable

is a legal term
unworthy of your fig basket.
It will not do
the job
except for the damnable dynamic
of exclusions
and there are only
reeds now
by the edge
of the element we jump in.

Love is all spirit,
how can one expend it?
Juice is but the ladle
as talk is the breath, unscripted
for the promptings
of the carpet.
Do you say rug?
So the fellah ploughs
with his Buffalo
before the surly sphinx
poor as his ancestors were
and its inheritors
when the line
of Thotmus ruled.
Those Chaldeans
children of our forbears
hasty nation of their Habakkuk
are forgotten now
save by local grey-beards
on staircases, like Dr Death.

I have ruffled
red velvet
’round my wrist
on the left side
with your pelmet
over the pillow in all bedrooms
where the naked fall
screaming for the grievous
selection of an order
or gazing outrageous
from palatial canopies.
And the empires
of Sardanapalus or Cleopatra
become grazing land
for nomad tribes, scribes
and editors
sacrificing ones
at the bridge
of some horizon
of the future—
fallow pinnacles
stuck skyward
cirrus-like in history
or the study of pleasure
and poetry
that era-
sure of letters
the ones which
kill the ones
turned into strangers.
Stick a knife into them.

Jappha, Persia,
Petra, Byzantium
are stirring phonemes
for romantic ears
now cut
from hearing.
The empires history
has conquered
in China
my grandmother's
yours and
the horn
recline their wreck
before us
like a bark
in which the Empirical
is laid out
in its cenotaph.
If you listen
carefully you can hear
the death-like rattle
in the throat
that murmurs millions.

As I write this
in the middle
—thank god for breaks—
of the King's bar
the Royal TV Society
is dressed
for evening.
Could they produce

more than US? Is Antony
Day Lewis here?
and Juliet
Binoche, to fail the
only screen test
of their lives? You were
always the
neufest pont
and I am
a Pauline celantro
spanned for walkers.
Did I
make you
laugh?
You know.
I do.
And so we are,
laughable,
and weep.

Your economy and our general
officers o'ertop some measure
or other
to explain this fall
right or glibly.
Supervisors talk
of trade routes, careers
and new territory
or peter out
in their poker chow
mapped for bibliophiles
of exhaustion

and Swiss gossip.
Yours make the night
perpetual
I will snore now
into eternity
so the mango
of something left
does lapse
what passes
for uselessness
to ensure the premises
are vacated —hard feet—
for the refurbished eagle
in fly-by time
appointed by the slate
wiped clean
of evening's pleasure
every night.

Our burning pages
were nothing
but beads
on a child's
abacus. Doubt the war
will always be.
Its abecediary
is more birth
certificate
than epitaph or vow—
a baby
lead by a crab.

For all our gold
lace and red
employment
all of our plumed caps
were not just
the sideboard
disguised
for dowry
of an inverse
now offered
like a ski-jump
to the future's bottom.

Are we
to become
tangled
in our plaques?
What, married
to our reviewers?
Seduced by the next
passing pip.
Now I
am laughing
because you went
for the inarticulate—
shunning the experience
the wit
or the stamina
of the recondite
lawdaughter, omrod,
huguenot, St Patrick—
galleries singed

a pore or two
in the drawn West
of marriotic folk
now ground
to gravel.

Why not?
So he guesses
he is the guest
of the future
present, if
guess there is
missing the apricot
sent perceptive
across tables
of endless bar talk
among the jostles.
Just to find it
amidst diurnal
stupidity
was happiness
after modernism
and we were
post-blessed
despite the false
love of kings
to lie above
the nation
in the neighborhood
of us all.

Forgive me
            I know
                        dogslife
when I see it
            and the cur
                        or bitch
must have work
            or her and his
                        trade will perish—
yours too
            empowered now
                        to erase
and invent
            memory and history
                        with the best
of them.
            That
                        was
luxury.
            So the fundament
                        dispends
saddened, echoing
            convinced
                        that human nature
is a poor thing
            remembering
                        the treasures
which rivalries
            of peoples
                        and forced arms
pennies
            in mud
                        or peat
have lost

to the world
come into
the garden
Magdalene,
and photographed.

We were
for once
the once
now lost
a statue
by Praxiteles'.
I am so
happy in a bar
full of people
especially those
who could benefit most
from the history
to be offered.
We will
never meet
the tailored limbs
of secondary BC
honeyed breath of Phidias
nor that bust of Hercules
which Nicetus speaks of
in Constantinople—
that that
the storms
rebuff.
Toohotwhotut,
Tootanktotoc,
Toowontutu.

But let us go
years hence
years hence
let us go,
let them go,
you can show me
the pool the Nassers
swam in
and the bar
and school.
The children
will be the same.
We will be
ornate with age—
reeds and serpent
discos
all about us.
And the swirls
that whip
by day
will fly by night
rewrapped
and issuing
in redder fabric.

With you the dimensions
of my fingers
were equal
to the waist
of womanhood
and you
were mannered

                    not as in the idling
                                        of a dream
but still
                    within
                                        a hearing
of the notes
                    and tones
                                        of the subdued chase.
We know in time's delta
                    these things
                                        become unimportant.
Statues, temples, libraries—
                    safety's belly
                                        gravely miscarried
for its future.
                    So there is black-suited
                                        laughter all about us
dressed
                    for broadcasting,
                                        not to be recollected.

I take you
                    to become this
                                        buying others
some of them
                    the hottest adornettes
                                        of your era
cruel as the claws
                    of the big cats
                                        posing
for Ptolemy
                    three thousand

wealthy curled darlings
at the race.
There's your back
garden
green
mauve
and sepia
sold in panic
unable to await
the future's tense
one always over
invested
in jumping.
So into the drink
we plunge
and buoy.
Remember how they rode
the horsey?
It softened
the whip with a smile.
The same go
forth to battle
and they fall
but falling
they're still victorious.

And though the field-hand
will leave
the field that he loves
though the smiths be ripped
from the forge
they burnt for

the weaver
abandon
her loom
the shepherd
the kid's knees
and his goats
or some squire the home
his fathers had squared
for centuries—for what
for a cheaper loaf
of bread
half a penny of love
less taxing,
a smaller domicile
to be buffed
across
one's own way—
the Architect
still sticks
by his sod
well bent
by her glass.
And the poet
like a lunatic
soldier awash
in his boots
cradles in her arms
a wet sleeve of rain
beside the vision
and memory
of an independent village.

That one so drinks
the jack
to change the tippling
of its territorial dung
Dr Loop is off
to Suede
and you
to Coventry or Cue
some collective discretionary
custody which
your myrmidons defend
to guard SUCCESS—
cessation that egress
suffers in the sex.

Damn words
words dam
wardens don
damn punishment
damn longing
for moreover.
Praise the surge
for loping
over again
the gut of tenderness.
Do not condemn them
for being
sorry to stir you
past stirring—
the pink plastic fork
remains in the tumbler.
I wish well

and well I wish
it is all
I can do: to question
always the knowledge
of human being.

When island nations
after glorious war
settle down to peace
taking a child
for a king or queen
the king marries
a wife or the queen
a consort
—unbeheaded—
then many
are the tricks
that breeding plays.
So there is pride, resistance,
ambition, the LA GYM,
waywardness
that sometime
did me seek.

Such chicanery
or thread
of pastoral
will spread
with callousness
to recoup

the feminine
    nineties while
        worlds burn like pages
signed or singed
    by two
        o'clock oil.
Or so the day
    comes through
        carelessness
pregnant, poor
    as the pair
        of the shoes.

We must be more
    than aware.
        Cities, letters
books, even love
    dies, crumpled,
        thrown to the bin.
But love does not
    die, that is
        the fathomless question.
And the answer
    is simply
        it does not.
We dream
    of our amour
        as we dream
of our birth.
    Some greene king
        continuous
is the ale master

all leading to lead
in first leaving.
Even while
the replacements
celebrate victory
the captives
are thinking.
Our daughters
will prophesy
all our memory.
It is enough.
They will learn
to circumvent
the gates.
The ghost of Ruskin
in the national gesture
treading on pyrrhic dreams
still damns
the generation
to banishment or Kent.
Islands of isolate
satyrs protect
the realm.

When I am old, bowed
bitter and laughing
with tough dog-fish
for an evening meal
I will think of this
or you – of that –
may I recall
amid the plaques

and tangles
my mother
sleeping in her chair
Selina at her
cushioned stair
Helen and left wing
in unrelated voice
on the darkened
landing. I have
the urge
but I cannot
say it. I will.
I will
though I know
that finally
it means nothing.
The words
are tissue (sere)
on erupting surfaces
stolen
from the future
and what you will
wear, unprepared
by the lectern—
what your ear
will hear
from this
throatless voice.

Grass and twigs
and bed
dreaming of lividness

the upholstery is bare.
Men tossing
on cots in prison
women preying
through the night
for sacks.

The Queen goes
springing on
her hydraulic subjects.
My druid colt
calls you to fit.
Weary of the branch
of slumber I am
nothing but yours
and you too are nothing
tangible—
surrogate, substitute
or nought
everything
eventually
dissembles.
The abdomain
rings in their ears
strange betraying sleeps.
Power seeking
force of liberty
high hatted
after concert lacks me.

Well there then now . . .
how are you
finally, lizardine
in the steamer
truncation of silence
at the rim
of the black list
number 13
sweetened for
mindfulness
determination
custodial orb
of ruined choirs
in little tails
mad gone
at the back gate
surrounded
by royal wagons
before the
initial yank, rousing
colonels from retirement
cherry's vested image
who knows not man.
Quite simply
one of
the adornments
inspiring words
thrown out
in the bar.
Stet tutores
at kin
letters leaving the world.

This like all
                great cataclysms
                                may be a lesson
of the passive future (eponymous)
                and our historian wonders
                                as she may wander
whatever should occur
                again. Women
                                who die for liberty
are Liberty herself.
                But no King is callous
                                except in literature.
There the beds
                enrapture
                                bengering.

The hands of gods
                were upon us
                                in the midst
of a bone-filled volley.
                And like the necessary
                                movement of our species
we rose and
                trekked, immigrants
                                who moaned and joined
burning colleges and baskets
                before the fireworks
                                at the great divan
or bed.
                St Mary's little trees still now
                                in the evidence below
wave their vision
                where the leaves fell.

In the King's toilet
—Who are you, sir?—
before the pea-green partitions
with a screwed hook
above the enamelled bowl
I reach for the metal
of the jeans.
Spilling out
the basins institutionalized
in mirrors
have nothing to say.
Their spigots
are shut.
Stainless steel
roll-tops
close the night.
Late night
surge continues
mouthpiece of proper time
strangers that sojourn
amongst us.
The push for freedom
exists in all people
vitally and
in some
even after they perish.

As you were
the patmost dweller
whose vision rang through
the spiralling room
so Jerusalem

whose destiny is to prepare
a bride or groom
for veils
can fill the newspapers
with a wall now, a wail
a soldier and a silencer.
Funerals follow
weddings and
precede them.
Muddy water is all
that spills
into a primrose sea.

Let the clocks and tutors
do it
to us then.
Harp I hear
a Nigerian king
who was born
of a camel driver
of Medina—
he got the Nobel
for dervishes.
The blind Irish beer
is nothing
but a rite of Swedenborg
and you. . .
You think now
above again
the warm throne
of a muscular kingdom.

When we were
in France
little songs were hummed
which boded neither ill
nor good
when kisses broke
the dam
then were
sullen thoughtful
walking
the bike
down Cranmer Road.
Souls of lovers
are bought then sold
for milk-fed infancy
for bays and
youth to slaughter
houses laid and beauty said
for a bit of bread
or thoughtfulness, endured
as spate on King's Parade.

Chuckling birds
are wilder than an English good.
At least in Paree or
Alexandria you could ponder
on the problem
actors of the glassine world.
And in Italy
there is always talk
murmuring in bed
beneath its gauze

the brace or breath
of cords and pillows.

Then bring me now
my bough of burning flame
my limpid arrows of desire
bring me my spear
my sheet, my morning key
my trinity of foot-filled May
for I shall not suit
this imagined wile nor will
my beeper sleep
in handsome
as do our letters
reappear, ripped from
Oympus now
pocketted, passed on
discarding the buried shard
of born condition
paper ceiling globe
of the little
push-pinned room.

While one knows
all gestures may be
futile in the end
one knows the red cap
of revolution will be
like Byron's
stocking in the sixth

of Harrow.
I know your children
will be at last
in spite of chance
abreast of change
progenitors of their right
no matter now
how plangent or penultimate
are the pleasures
of this lamp or ink.
I deserve nothing then
but this stolen
end of sure sedition
nailed by periods
mottled with the cream
contemptuously discharged
at the Assizes
by cretins cast.

But memory. Memory
memory set down
remonstrance verify
the family leaving.
You will have married
talking like a pen
lost now for spoons.
Our bought tobacco
inhaled up late
only the linear stage
of rolling trade
yours for mine.

                                        Who but doltish folk
would think
                    my beggar
                                        mine?
Turned by the logic
                    of the day off
                                        of some guy in the moon.

This record is a record here.
                    The other course
                                        is the course
of mothers and fathers
                    sisters and nincompoops alit
                                        while hearts and hats
lie mouldering
                    at most a parking lot
                                        a table caught
in the scotch
                    of generation
                                        market heaven
Herzegovina and willows
                    weeping little
                                        St Mary's picnic nap
over bodies planted,
                    some blasted need of annihilation
or your majority
                    some blanch of nobody's
                                        bunch of roses
leaves us benches
                    for our lunch
                                        at marketplace

what stuck
the stuff
in mud.

Now I hear you coming
down the shadowed
sward toward me.
Courage
my dear
courage.
Now I feel nothing
turned around
toward something
slimmer
a muffled cry
in bloom
an apple tree
a churchyard.
No pin, tie or safety
embodies us
can fathom it
though age become
a studied radiance
pushing hard
through the cotton.

Dark head of willfulness
delicate breathing
white face of red.
When did you

get fat?
I think it is
the copse drops
everything we gots
down into the streets
below
and the rain hails
sleet and snowdrops.

Then bullocks nick the vice
at the King's bridge
and kick a paper ball
past Gardenia's
to color the eyes and yes
oppose the nose
tinned sandwiches at the backs
before May below
all say goodbye
to Madame Joy.
All leaves
the rolling music
'round the room.
Everything
that's vaseline.

Everything heard
unseen. All leaves
the mistaken spell
red paper camellias
twisted and looped for all

so cool, so calm
so cold, so curled
traditional.
Laughter about the bottle
that's come to leave
forgot to stay
the sere unfurling
unlearnt endurance
that loves to love
to say *O*
hello to pitch
dark keyless music
in the father's phantom
sleep beside sort song
mattress and fire escape
room to kneel
sheet to sink
scotch knackered
in the nomenclutch.

Though I have the feeble body
of a woman, I have
the heart and mind
of Kings.
Then, there, born back
into the street
the light glows nightly on
in the office
or the home
garden and alone
abroad and there
abandoned and adorned.

Eyes and nose and jacket
at the hook and stoop
night goes lightly off
no one for now
at home.

Lounge suit and gown
charged for dessert
through the tear
at the King's back
yellowed by fellows
at the southern edge
of the field of rape
grown for sheep
and the division of villages
towns and counties
burning pages
in an aberration
twice in line
to be writ third
reflected once in glass.

Ring the bell off and on.
Author and authorities
authorize.
Balance afloor
the ceiling
is all.

No one

to fill the camber

alone and well

together and at last

no one

at last

at home.

Winter 1993/1994

ANSWER TO DOCTOR AGATHON

ANSWER TO DOCTOR AGATHON

We are tired of your socage rates
and your tiresome imitation of intellectual property.
We're tired of your dreary sough
of Vergilian fortitude
strained through Corsican manners
without the hard stuff to back it up
except for some waxy grotesquerie
of the child-like dance of death.

Your presumption—like a bell without
a clangor or a fag without its mouth
filled though it be with its moiety
of the divine afflatus or is it
the pork in the barrel
interloping pony
showing grandeur when the intensity is gone
from the charge to the quasi Mongolian hill
more than apparent (well nearly apparitional)
that attendance at the feeble till of knowledge
now oversubscribed officially
and underfoddered
for the young guardians of the secret
whose cell-like trance of pure ovation masks
an anxious umpirage of ums and ohms of unofficial conduct
so the winsome rider takes the practical note and remembers
to go by—Gibbsy imaging—
and the uninvited guest yahoos the empty seat
of knowledge and continues forgetting
to rack it up to scratchers

and their tireless approximation of ticking
                                        pricking lists unravelling
to sex, gossip and all that other stuff that seeps
out the teddy when you chew on its leg too much
        —was that a mind field or a sloggy fen?

Or was it some unregistered rabble the hillocks contained
in cans of film where Yanks play Brits playing shook-foil or
the aventurine with gold-colored inclusions and little seeds
rich with oil and sloped against
                                                the edge of the corral
where the horses bolt with seas and manes more fiery
than the Hittites multiply.

                                        Nor could it stand analysis on a pinhead
'round yon private feast of thoughtful canapes
nicked by mates and their material before the mess
without the message can get up
                                    and sweep out with yet another Tennyson
who wouldn't recognize Voltaire if he moved to Finland
Station or drank with Montgomery Cliff
                                                    who died the same
day I did, but no one could expect someone without vows
        to know that
any Wednesday evening before the bash
that crashes through the brain with its quotidian pain
gone stale before the theoretical onrush in the fold
                                    of ones superiority to ones superiors
                                        and they are like gods!
Oh well, it is always more than this and less than that
and tomorrow's sash will fix the lawn wounds with its rain
                                                and only Plato among the Greeks
was smart enough not to pass up a good time
                                                        and drink the dawn

'til red-eyed enough to know the strangers
from the estrangement
and the dumb show for what it was—
the transparent queue of the local
calling the recruits to sign on for the salty marshes
to be royal caballines of unutterable protection
witnessing the seminar remains
nearly Elizabethanate in their adornings.

And it's such a lilackey time of year
no wonder the excess is so virtual
no wonder the slides break down and boats
melt into tears at the locks—the animals
high-heeled bouncey mentors of dementia and the swan
sung news which the muse deducts, and Duncan Grant turns
into a chicken and the discriminations
and no irony is so ironic
as the irony which faces mean
to see
or seem to mean
like Victor Hugo's ghost
striding to the hilt of Dreyfus in another cell outside
where there is nothing to do but love the microbicide
of the philippine when it comes at last
smelling of pleats, almonds and the deciduous dew
instead of this completely sexist dramaturge
that's brown of shirt and swelling in the Goetheneum
quite striking in the proprieties where the statue of the Rose
is buried, and political economies declare it inappropriate
for a ballerina to wear a tutu in the Common Room
of seigniority even in a painting—
de-accessioned to the cellar
with the wine, caved in to an appreciable maturity where

the blooms swaddle in a nest of keys
though nicely benighted
not to say very bright, not to say another tiresome imitation
of blatant reaction to the nod's thatch
infringing
on freedoms any schoolboy would scotch
to no surprise
though I suppose they get release
what do we really know of the Supposes, especially
those which pass for brains when the gatekeepers pass out
the sheets, the tickets, the letters and the sheepskin
and experience in the writ is validated
for Time's publicity instead of the heat
of History which the marbles crush
or the deconstruction of the truly marvellous.

In the bluster at the sunny end, those chippy
enough to be born and grace the choir books
with their palms, to be read
as the emblazonry on school-felt crimson flaps which pass
with Emmanuellian seal (is there anything left of 1994
which can be said to be Emmanuelesque?)
grim humours
brimming from the gang of fortunate seekers after knowledge
sex, memory and a rumour—
more an unofficial bundle
of twigs which Geoff or was it Liz laid it on one night
was the root of fascination *and* fascism
well maybe just the Bund friends make
better dictionaries at least
than any old regular
academic group heading for the drink.
Anything remotely resembling a walking grove of trees

better get cracking.
Wedding marshes await them
but who could be hip to that?

To go no more
aroving
heads and cheeks pass by
to such discretion
so discrete
and so proprietary to the appetite
like running for psychological office
and we are sure you will be elected ASAP
by your secret constituency and so

A toast—to Sylvie!
graduand as mutable as a race, a gender
or a sexual memory
leaping from punt to bobbing punt
in a welter of naughtiness
in her white thing
from Cancer Research and wearing blithely
the cashmere of the soul like an entire navy
of adoration conscripted to be yours
while to be sure
others just need a little space from which to speak
some good to the good, well bully for them
and bugger Plato I want God
and I desire him in the form of a woman please
for equality's sake and the tickets—
another birthday in the tam and bun shop of a cloud
instead of this repetitive cleansing
program which nicks people and their things and we
stand and fall with any who cannot unofficially be scrubbed.

So see what you think
Queen bee, little bear
bouncer at your appointed Agathon's Feast
and depict the view.

O look! the animals stray
rivetted in place—and argylls sing.
I suppose you must have these chirpy little meetings
to lord over them so you can become cleverer
than before
perching at the edge of Pythagoras
with a worm in your mouth
like a hawk of the times
but you have no idea
Simonides
what is happening or what has happened
to Susanna, myself, Queen E or the contraries
now that there are swallows disallowed
to be nest or furrow or hostages—
nor how it will be recorded beyond.

But your try-out for Alcibiades
was a success and you are cast
in the role before the troops
be assured
in the next lull in the battle
don't worry you'll be great, only a Queen Bee
and with such a voice can approximate
the little bear we have in mind.

There may be no chance left
to change

no ashes left to memorize the same
Your bossie blowsiness is ceremoniously pumped
and we like pumped
preferring not
to neglect the opportunity to stand on ceremony.
But if you had a dog
I suppose
we could get it to bite us
or reconceptualize it as golden curls at our heels
but you have no garden and you remain
a flowerless fellow
in the end you are indeed as cold and just
as layered as your wax.

But we only love the sun, the violent universe
and the return to redness that is the manifesto of feeling.
And in that realm my dear Simonides
you do not even speak
like a whisper—
Antigone's broad Thessalian sunhat
worn by a horse.

Yrs

Trimalchio
6 9 94
Cantax

[last conference of Unofficial Knowledge, 1994, Cambridge]

ARABESQUE AT BAR

ARABESQUE AT BAR

what I sack is the knot in the rush

ARISE
tin Lizzies
who adore
the wooden beam
and dim apensicolar
harbingers ashore.
Glad call thunders
from the faggots
and your arabic
chain and ore
vile bondage
of adornoboys
what Britons will
the clitheria
of liberty fear
with a cold
hand and
an insensible mind
miff the muff
the Russian canes required
which blooms
buried lost
with your fair
tutu skein.

UNREAD ears upside of other
check the savage vowel
which dare not speak
or name satyric
red vermilion
as bundles
deposit zeroes
at the motley
bed or bank
balls on these cravats
guesses ribbons stream
I say welcome again
the breast
of the caprice
and fall
to question questions
depraved madonna
claps to any
conference
of sex
with knowledge
and stuff
like that
and that.

BEAT me with carbon black
red at top to lick
scratches back to veil
what superciliates
another arching
glance backward

no better than apples
    of the chasuble
        night hiding
dear cherry's diction
    before unholy families
        demand it to be theirs.

SO the certainties
    leave their charms
        to market passage
prosecuting nature
    minds to mould
        the burning wicker
desire lost
    as basketting fire
        licks to being
the aberration
    what colors
        us merry.

HELLENISTIC willy
    nilly to some
        pale approximation
of thee
    —torrid zone—
        that birds
the bridehead
    to its eager

liquid lustre
anon and again
fucking the A
at the alabaster.

TWILIGHT infringement
last dawning
gardenias shrink
to twist Bronzino
to t-shirt shrift
mildest mixture
too slow
the speeding
of Kings farouche
from day
to nights reuniting
les amants
trading frequent
flier miles for degrees
of fading pleasure
in successive flight
slowly born exact
enough at quayside
leaping to the paper globe
overskirted dressing gown
shaving cream
xeroxed and collated
champagne till pride
disdains the flush
and returns it
sigh
for sign.

BUT mirror stand aside
                    recruits remaining
                                        pips that pass
fellows preferred
                    for stories
                                        scars assured
courtyard portraits
                    paper memories
                                        periodic orals
declining love
                    banked to rest
                                        a mild suicide.

SO mank the tent
                    baggages drum and trumpet
                                        girls beat and blow
into Ste Anne
                    glasses seducing
                                        the sequestered city
lads agog at home
                    with whiskey cloistered
                                        from the populace
lingering hours
                    they got poured
                                        and pissed into them
good till empty
                    bottles them
                                        part way to spring.

Nell 'ambiente
turn them over church keys
they're good and done
weary them to sleep
with fierce caresses till
brutal spasm prove
the plan for climax
cunningly achieved
on bottom's snorting dream.

FAUX Britain
never certain
but ever there
primitive in reserve
overweening virtue
in the royalist
tampaxation of her tongue
princely happenstance
croqued into grace
into serviceable lamps
wickets nodding fornices
gasping uncouth
in surly time
beyond measure
or delight
for any
aide-de-camp
who fattens
pouting lips—
for thee
Doxie Swallow.

CHASED fearful
        to the gate below
                my ass
braying rayban
        yelling midnight
                noise surpassing
the complete duration
        such din sustained
                ridden riot elongated
as will sever some
        membrane shocked to seal
                the bargain seamless.

THEN moving down
        still coming not
                with unguent swing
they root they swill
        they sling they hog they swerve
                they tie it tiny
slowly in the sinking swoon
        dying like a vat
                which stills in stirring
they lapse again
        waves still crimson
                ’til looped in rolling
back to be back again
        codified in twining
                soft divan or bed.

NOTHING quiet
will be quiet
finally in the end
enveloping them
pelisse, pelmet and recompensed
at fools' moon
memory passed
where Dr Raw
puns upon sunup
bathes everyone all
to be somewhere there
the dansant rising
at briney charge
of plunge again
scrubbed again
undressed further even
by art to become one again
or some multiple two
of clock oil
artifice of thee
unofficial turf.

TO sap Stephanotis
past Chlorodyne
leaving limbs
leaving arms support
the rise of kingdoms
greylight folios
fury exploding to
smouldering shrubbery
sip the fragrance

tipped on nails of flesh
slip the trace
of trembling favor
able at the seat
of pools and jays
wile huguenots away
one sultry afternoon
and evening
hour unabled
to refuse the trembling body
of its jumping fast
table leaves Temple
which even song even time
refulgent cornbashers
will not exonerate.

THIS married psyche
well mounted tigerish
to the other
and laid her down
the rest deserted
for cunettes
to take the current mill
fulmine throttle becks
and humps
to hem to haw
hurtles thrown
at splash
of regulating
daybreak splice
and sink to splurge.

NO wonder all
the players broke the zone
no odds were greater
unloosening bands
to saunter back disgraceful
and deck the angle
boys ablaze
within their splendid domes
where ignorant armies
her terror can't assuage
nor redden fervor to
the soothing power
which couches hurl
like ski-jumper from ski jump
nondescript which broke
the qualifying run
when they were you know where
unpredictably two one comes
to careen
what is around
rump fed senate house
repossessing trembling
tenderness at the rim
of nadir V.

NEUTERED deep
at the back door
and within
where rose
conceived
the sting tip

and pricked
reluctant fear
brief suspension
centered at blushing
open murmurring cheeks
brinking submission
midnight oils checked
clamor applauded
heads careered
by applause triposted
opening veins
to enlargement
small as lashes blackened
from pretzels curling
opisthograph poppies
doubling the nerves
racking limbs
to identical lens
of lovers twinned
cup driven, emptied
of duplicities.

PROVENANCE for the other
minute spending
the way in
studious manoeuvers
course tested
for the purse
futures bet to lit
elbows burnt like wagers
little punts jumped

swerving pivot
wobbling essayed
in seminar remains
invited by engraving
appointed envelope
to be unsealable
heeding seizure
at the surface
wild lamp beneath
rubbing comes
sailing to the floor
revealing palimpsest.

DEEDS which fountains
splash to cheer the surd
unbearable horizon
brazen sun
unbereavable unity
until spalding
beachy head again
or skying linen
in its habitation
high above
Doc Martens kicks
at hostels of regina
stupendous bottom
chained subliminal
and channel reared
half tunneled to never
mariners awash with French
risen every morning

halls reclined
to see to cry
divan designs
tootling the chemise
which only Fanny
rocks and seas.

OR Fancy hears
and stretches forth
arms to four
strange limbs
and stranger hours
albeit the smallness
of awful vast
concussion writ large again
around going down
where smelts dispend
thick with blood
and lord dark red
the wings left rippling
to the level beam
lips erected
islets intertwined
dug quiver darted
shores adrift
ere's melting brood
meridian joined
fresh choughs
and daws (liger)
turfy crests
unhound to flag

nicely beat to slump
      perhaps to drowse
            flocks and figurations
cut to sheet stains
      angular canvas
            and rouse cerulean view.

WHERE butts the crispy
      till dimples day
            dissolution sloped
to shift and buoy
      fixating modern ecstasy
            to a statement
not startling it.
      Tenured is the night
            and the divulgences
slaughtered to young
      whispers old with bearing
            sweet anonymity away
and its soon ripped
      twenty three
            dissolving fragments.

SO give us back
      our dearest father's arms
            and I will promise
to arm them once again
      against brides
            fellows, starlings

unfulfilled
apricot singular of series
absent rumors
false echo alarms
dispelled at once
missing sinking periods.

THIS reigning tumult
in a tranquil rain
where bosoms sorrow head
phantoms agitated once
held rapture apposite
melting tears severe
to dissuasive airs
subletting heaven
for a damasked chair
with which to watch
what night will wear
warning porters
legend to the lees
blatant warm or wild
one morning hour
maintenance was worth
two there unlured
by thought or matrices
to peter out
or shine the mud
lies under iris skies.

JEALOUS hands on Catullus
throbbing disregard
of glances to be fleet
peeling back the glue bits
pacts of luminous night
germinal termagents
subsuming the doom
of cowardice
and treachery.
Brahms concertos
cannot gainsay
these casements
nor erase omradically
the ultimate errant
Keynesian economies
which count the hours
years correspond to seconds
burnt as ruptured things.

STILL hovering
palpable as a pleasure
memory's illusion
culled to fade
in the annointment tilted
joining titles
bursting globes
blown to dawn
switched to on.
Call the veil
call the responsibilities
animal bodies

made to influence
the second sense
repulsive to the whispers.

THRILL on
dash of lines.
Still come
innocent criminal mix
span still
the limbs
delicious death
which train
the disembarked.
No ruby ring will still
Venetian clamors end
or finger better furze
nor thumb the furry flower
but your wet rings best
treacled with their hair
reaching for the real
career unspelled
that beds the backs
stop artlessly *auto fatale*
at the edgy island
of this stationhood. . .

for Jennifer, Steve, & Elizabeth
Memorial Day 1994, Providence

MON CANARD

12/25/94-1/1/95
44, rue Lepeu, Paris

In the name of Bacon, will you chicken
me up that egg.
Shall I swallow cave-phantoms?

How rich she smells
This abortion of a fledgling!
I will eat it with a fish fork

MON CANARD

Julie my duck, mama's lute, chouchou in lieu of amore
of our loo, butte of my butte, beaute of your butt
mont rue, my verity former not HERE, not her
mob spent of row, flowers in rue Lappe, pet asinine pot
my lovely cinder, mine ashen heart, onliest wit
ness to my witness, jump in Seine, berth, ankleberry
every thin necklace nested, sturdiest hysteria, white
patent leather policefemme, unreading gaoler, op
pen opera, princess mon amie electuary Jew, petit rat burg
er, my choo choo, coughdrop of my esophoguy, my lu
dens, by my mitten, minion of my invisible cake, liz
ard die of my destiny, mutt, cuff, flycast, gal
oshes, SMITTEN GLOVES, smith of my smith, bull
's blood drawn in sleepy smiles, petite carotide
mine outside of libraries, mine inside of sky, re
flection of a flicker, intermittent heaven, ce jour triste
lourd de lassitude, she there what's her name, little beachym
sham, damoiseau mar on my divan, penny couch
my virtual chum, chinchin of my chin, chin duster of
my shoeshine, main cat pal, pause, GAUGE, going on
wobbly but unmusty, extra key, coin, ma chatte for
an hour and a life, terminal initial of Lucrèce, Lucretius
place where my fingers learnt their place, ex sexy gerun
diva, my rue de la main d'or, liberty burning anklecuff

dearest ear, l'oreille cassée, nose for my eyes
agreeablest knot, sweet tooth, toot, my b
low, my job, my WIFE, my snow, wasted poplin of un
closed drawers, knicker of my let, my tie and
my redundancy, tongue of hyacinth, tongue of clement
een, plane darkling, unlasting loan, my loonie
st tune, noon of my noon and the second afternoon all
night, sheet kneeler, slat breaker, my color
less felt seat of Leicester's DOUBLE life, shag rug and
shadow of my digression, a new vague shape of day, fig
ure e'en now at nightie, my little porcelain tiger
passoire, that jump from and for the rest, the mother lip
in sync, shortest contraction, resignation from science
and slow time, assent, decline, premier something or other

something of an aberration, paper fire, sno
ring goddess, ray MOND and grace, arc of my curve ta
page too fast but who was driving, leg woman and
like my wood breast, felt of your drawer, draw and match
of cards, eclipserer, queen NUMBER third at the fir
st second, contract, con, bouncing hat, alter e
goes red tickets, gravid nun, posh nutter of my sundae
nouvelle retrovert, my disability, her name, her beat
rice, golden sectioned two year old, unread
ie champ at the edge of the OVAL, oh drunken race
novel absence, arching is a bell borne away
to Kings PARADE, testimony to the rule of chance, balls
cupped in hand, sweet nadir V, my playing
chump, muddied boot, dye of our rhetorick in

sincere rôle, my sack in the morning, sack
at night, hanging round, your hanging over, come bloom
ed hangover, now lapse at last, your jump in can
tax, womb of her own, CHAR at my back, tramp
of time, cave lamp, conundrum, shirt, garter, high
absence curled in me girl, my admission to literary so
sighty, skin of Dame Edith, curled darling of my sove
reign unit, NATIVITY, my incensed franc, far
thing nearer to the bank than PILLOW puffed and
fluffy on the sheets, able Irish rose which Tuscany re
turned, just ex-kant, wait to come, way home
boy, my fatigues, lasting past the LAST exaggeration, I woman
bella bella, Lady Baloney stript ease there, Dr Death
ly silence, my well, my sill, wall, morphia kristakis, my now

my then, my there, me shaddoh, me shallow, khan uke
chanookie of an NC Hudson, O BAY, wan ass braying ewe
ramification, bronze niño, prefect lapel, school pin
of John Adams, up the wazoo of music murals, la fa
mine fed utterance, Titian, heterogenous dendron
age, homogenous polynomial young or old, O FMN, effeme
haine, paint faced self-portrait, unwrit eddieface, E
vidange, ending evidence of scent, sleep above rest below
whistling powers leaving in little tunes you HEAR playing
just below surfaces walked through, bed 'n' breakfast
one, unpractised theoretician, Falmer miscalculant
sleepy comma of my snood, CAMPANION, some sense in water
colors of white space, other, lover, liver, puffed ottoman
mother, written basket, unborn bastard, pharmaceutical cropper

brother, not her, not here and here then out of ear
rings, shot, heaven pendulant and leavening to rise to do
ugh re mi false soul, Tito, ma tétinesse, sister hymn
ast eleven year-old songbirds mistook for ignoram
o ruse, manner ADDER to my discordant fig, psalm
ist in the wild, earnest Nilus, flyblown palm, ab
horrence of recruitment, not theirs, but near
ly blonde, virile haggard, wild salvia, spit
of my suze tip, sloopie dogg dog, dream-lidded eyes, 3000
pound cement friend, ashes to DHL, nose for yes
IBM femme, squeeze, eyes for knowing holy colander, salad dew
my daze, my twist, my gig, my gaze, my digs, bulbous poppy
fair couscous, famishment, ma femme, saved to be ma
chine rigmarole, bellicose vein, STCD, old fodder sea otter

such folderol of benger fief, karma sutured to a ragged arm
anonymous mouse, eros restored to tyre
s and to juice, tissue of outlasting periplum, the e
lectrice, eaten trees, feast, little piece electra
less, treatise in the shadow, my JEANS, ziggurat, sor
ry islander of this flung night within yon galeforce
flight, rememberer of stories, burning page
or match or GAZ, ism of my jazz on the prominent rock
of your roll right into First Court, then seconding
number in end, nothing SAID, stiff pinky, nothing did
o'er my inability to tell the past part from the present
s you mistook for belongings, itemized allegories
call list to leeward, belonging in your organizat
ion, airie cigaret, corporelle, bodice of emolument

embodied dead end reese's cup, bodiless sybarite, m
other's maw, Daddy's back, young warder of warning
awesome morning WHACKER, tillage pill of contraception
pyramid point, tomb of rapture, little tummy dumpling, cul
de sac, handlebar, nicked bullock of former vice, chance
lore kept for your adornment, i.e.'s black umbrella to me
Biblical tie on recenter bellies, seamen semen's
seaman's semen, TOLSTOY'S old yellow moose and weather
not your red pocket book, purse, engine, bin, my rail
ing weeper, bank, pillow, reservoir, O my river, streaming e
gad falling heaven, whippersnapper HABITAT divan, whispering ho
mardi rhetorician FULL of tutors, debits, Chiracuterie at the hotel
de ville re: mover to the floor, movie hand in pocket, my little un
boilt lobster, sunshine, heliogabled lawn, plummy load

star, only sunshine but the sunshine, savage little sal
mon, enlargening salamander, my punk, my house, my thou
sandy little RAVINGS of sister at stairwell, Doctor Raw
big hiphopper hipper than Louise or Penny but youth
ful prone to both, pin-daring Corinna, jostling pye
off the trolley twin, last lashes to lack me, image poring
singeing porridge, raffish cut, your honeyed breath, our tailor
ed limbs, nodding rododendron, bobbing face in glass, eddie
faced first poem at bar, masking placemat at MARKET PLACE, inspi
ration's minute note on tragedy, crying Rachel's sister Bologna, number
than telephones, leaving that leaves the mistaken word, jollity
left for laundry and right of my unblessed leave, a
wol gol darny and waving from the No. 12 LONDON open-back
washed of my Indian shore, seas' oblivion, seal's wide spin

drift gaze toward paradise, bark voyager, see
Di roam, tub set off on an empty sea, fet
ich, trophy dress on Lisa's wall, loss to FETTES, ross
all of my startling after birth, monstrous weep
ster, stirring SISTER, little goldencurl of
St Gabriel, flown bird, my same one, c'est
moi, and guardian of my heart and sole of my mort
ality, teetering at brick wall, tottering statement
chasm of career, child of your surgeon, morning
after pill, sweet STINKIE, my deeper sinker, bet o'er
rivers of blood, whispering ear, charmster at chasm of
first love, secondest yank of gare de l'est, regard
at last idea of US, and remember your age, our
agency and the others', jealous mud in springtime

pint of beer, sandy bottleneck petering out, burning
minute menilmontant, sturgeon, quarter, caca boudin
puppyshiite, POOPIEDOLL, nut, hog, whole wet knick
er, stocking Christmas, mote in middle dis
tance, crystal night, scored pan, much good, that H
that was a T, eaglest lectern of the King's chapel, pre
tenderest bride of cathedral night, EVEN my song, my
lyric on your jacket sleeve, breast lapel, eyelet gauze, pro
scription, stylish vinyl, broken loud speaker, stylus ex
pensive record of oracular day, by night my minute, dyna
mite G 'N' T drinky mate, burning aberration, fiery ration
al nub of butter, thigh queen, raCONteuse, fringe tour of noon
mon histoire, love that loves to love to love to
turn the King of Clubs, rabbit and bird for ben laden

to live, little scholar recumbency recoups, gonest gr
and mother, Gonna, big shot at the little pond
of Queens, duck! my frank, incense murmurring
smoky robed one, prefecture of the GLOBE, your count
ess parson may not recognize but hear, honest
est recoverie, luminous numismate, oraculaid
vocabulet, TOILET schweppes with closet porridge, port
age of my nonny white plum, please, my gat, miasma sh
ort, colossal fornicatrice and the matrices all souls
weight, rupture's <rapture> vice versa, O clef of my ro
man, center radius to later Georgian age, Gibson Girl, erupt
ure of such mécanique, waiting solely for the Virtual Finn
meaning justified only marginally by CONTENT indented to
last, decadentest soirelle, you wish, my vision to see

the first rye bread of our grandchildren delayed to
their majority, deux oui, MINOR key for the major mass
Cambridge my ass, Galveston, cantarabian palomino
packed bags cantaxian, crane grooming crones to be
crooners, giver of births better than alphabets
bed of waves, my doigts on those gambols, your digits, wolves
devoted to Caius, new territories, okiedokiest proxy for an S
and M occasion, lover of the Egyptian period, kid, milk
er of my dolt, chamois, carolling on MAS CAYOL, more pa
nana than ever gone, two moms, NEZ pierced, Queen Squaw
King babe, first of my second, seconded once 11th hour, my fir
st, QUEEN E ticket, yon cancelled ton and a half pound voy
age, suit, pants, settlement, and my instructions to the jury lad
dies 'n' reddlemen, overlook honor courts, your charges

dismissed, kangaroo sextant, my courtship, oh no, lares and pen
ates, St even vie ROSY, prosaic loser, industry, un-deux-trois, mon troi
sième trouble, first first second afternoon, nec
plus ultra terrorist with a spoon, a pastor and a past
ure, at no kin of any king of mine, two-one a bit wobbly
on marriage, like all the best, will you, NUMBER at the end of look
see London, think prose, my librarian, stirred moth before the fire
y Senate House stars, then what dust, conspirator of posted DEVON
CREAM made oak older than a Roman hedge at Dortminster, lacan
ic canneloni of Naples call key babe ogled by the double
breasts of harrowed Shropshire LADS, more bengerer than Hardy
more stern than twain, swifter than a speeding bullock, dark
wit more gill than beer, more germane, and better in the but
lery than upon a ferry pausing in the chanel nightshade

passing pissing death too close and reading closer enroute
to its demise in straight man's line, skewered by designer jeans
a lurker columned to HANKY appointments in the tutelage
we see the die is cast, light out, Dadie dipped, COUCH Doc Krack
ow marred royal periods replete with consanguinity and sang
froid unrecognized conspirator, midnight special, slave bed
spread, black virgule per termagent behind, woman of no
one, but too one and onlie, snows somewheres there
lumina nocte, may geese gander the gender at last, car life-saver
lean at the roundabout, midnight at NOON, gland-born helicopter wreck
awning seer, fifteenth of February and fifth form greene ears, idol
a tress of divorced Kings, petite jouvencelle, united manquess
more lovelace than swift, but tuck quicker than speedmerchants
academic Philly, Getty, Charlotter in Boston, try coven

try gentlest woman privileged to know luxury at last over
added total, sum with selection, don demoiselle, fly
my night by day, lamp down dawn go-to-school, inter
dicted to be stationary, TOSSED-OFF letter, my little master
bater O all the time, well be lief that is left, unjailed reader
red DRESS unaddressed, interdit jour et nuit, ma bête
noire, rim midi, demie raconteuse, ma con kissed
adored, English rose, seducer of Attila, to be or not to be
headed poésie, hollow ferns in her hair, em am pa ok ma
own lie bleeding, ombre PMS, parturition and perturbation van
quished pause, believe them then, my entry, involved new men
net over hair and vulcanized for the photographers
hallowed furnacies, mon JACO bin, nubbin florin, chaté, pene
tration of colonies' reluctance, nudging assent, met ta

blette admittance to the kernel, married Marilyn, balt
ic amore, regent, horn, mon père, hotel opposite toy
store on FIFTH Ave RITZie, my St. Regis, removed pre
servation of candies, scruples, candles, scotch at posted wind
ow east of Central Park, where JFK sweet talked bombshells,
van of tennis balls, cloudy drawn ghost riders on Skye
white Vanna who flips the letters, macadam blazing
Butterfly of the ping pong table, CAMBER weller of we
were all beautiful once, onset of transatlantic turban, prat
crit, clothes treading, quit of my arms and ARMOUR of my mantle
transcripterasing cellular telephase of sectarian cell division
sweeping up to Bristol to bathe, baa baa Bathsheba of dumbster
Oak, argument of the Knesset, MS spelling of he and thee the
she of it, Babylone Shiite, sensational ideation of kumquat at Spalding rut

ate something sensational like the mind of a shark, ague of Jackie E
mail, little carp, jack et jour, tracks open to clouds and ALL but cap
rate married instead to elle or toi or just a baby in this business
of love, his Julia, whose robber was that, my cacaphasia
be an animal, be beast of the theater of offspring, like crickets' knees
though you were my ORCHID, 500 miles from this TTTown, those hun
dred locks Shakespere wilts at halfway house, reader poorer than win
dow breeze, more curious than strong, soft you, teeth acquired on cob
webs in the gap, lengthening tears and sorry tales whispered
lark spurned dawn, love, mind brains' lack of tape, overused pause
button, prepinned aura, flush, sin, pluperfect prefect's badger cour
tesy of John Smith, May's anthology whip and actress, rôle and dharma
turgid in one dead eddy of the CAM, where yon private punts
be curbed, jacks, dreamless Priam, Helen, plum Aegisthus, JHPed

whose sum of sorrow nectarless at the seat of vibration neat
expedites the proem equinoxed mute and luminous and asleep
o'er marketplaces, BUNTING bed, island ward, frontrunner to be
or nut, rod, staff, zuza, suz philippic, weep and drew, lash
me calendar, ridicule lush life, cindered crawfish, CAESURA upend
ed carpet day, John coked diem, old Vietnamese courtesan of mine
assassination 3 weeks on, Stella Mathews, strikerest after pen
ultimate Henriette, bobbie more, moor worth more put-out, with
ered heights or MINI pearl, where'er medicine goes goest thou smarting
who late shows states sere vice, moaning white tales, black
tie coming off it, grown NUTS for infancy, for bays, for Venetians
jet some who set this down, enforced halfway incestuous adult
erer, swell wish to set you free, but castle keep abreast, car
pet of my echolalia, chiclet essence of gin with turbocharge

singing naked on ginseng coverlet at pane, O limp pied
pus, seer, wing, sore foot of my snore store, eaten puce of
soupçon, dough-like pain, chortled LAIT, my hung and light thought
bespoke obscenity hungry for things, timeless woman
possessed and prepossessed in time, Antibes, that Athens we did love
loss to culture and the nomenclutch, cool turgid gain in Norwège or in
Suede pregnant BABY of paternoster row, my what's-her-Ph. Deed
butler's battle, mud cop, under eager rod and Christian ghost tome
to me fate, fire of peat moss, my fulsome Kate, Helen's horse trumpet bl
own your John, sirène, shackled Ulysses on a CHERRIED mast is
a bell who sent to see, cemented sea shadow, robins, azaleas, discover anew
finland, sangfroid knell moi, grinning amiably Churchill like Lucy Cha
nell, note and TONE greater than jazz or savage, ma savane cuivrée
future's routine, grave tomorrow unquiet as mercury, nun barely bell

bearing daily, excuse and chevrolet, greatest fucking phaeton of let
wet lawn, rolled everyday and rocked 600 years, my dear, metal
licked replacement of DR DEATH'S stony passage, my replacement
the replacements, traceries of little dicker meant or razed, tar
get tempted meaning, marked and edited for reams of unwrit letters e
mended by subsequent nature unresponsible to silence and the sloughing
of slow time, intimate sequence with quasi syntax, only intimation
information and immortal tally in the bursar's book, launched at
Bloomsbury, ELLELUNCH at Magdalene, vague novel of this nouvelle
vague, kissy idiote, senile whispers' sycophants, queen of the adornments
fuser of refuse and sect of this vice-pro, picnicked academician born
once our listener now your Queen, arabellesque bridehead
potted philopena, hock in heed of ham kneeding her, Rubenesque altar
ego bound to don Peter, mon mon-sieur le Prince, my brolie's E

lector in vigilance, Dante beat pin getting dumber and full
er by the minute, number SAFETY intermediates determine nation
in a minute—space between strokes and strophes— blue lutes
a future evening in New Haven or Philadelphia, staid up-late
sister citizen, proof of the pudding and of phenomenology's up
start reluctance to be immediate, misunderstood or MS under
standing, ins closet, up against the wall, shaking the hall
tree, leaping cashmere doe-like at PICKERAL, punt to punter's punt
left and right and about face, harbinger banger of the pint
sized tear in cream-shaved dressing gown, distance and lily
pro-sacked of pro-choice, the saxophonist's compensatory labor
a try, SEA heart thought skate, approximation of the fens about-face
xeroximation of Roxanne, Martha Ray, Stephen Hill, and bee afield
champêtre's sleep before the last days of Socrates' only hem, he mal

locked as the graduand of Flaubert's parrot and this petite conun
drum, dim sung fury into that goodnight, window of Wales and Herod
prepuce floating in the SCRUM off Hydra, reluctant to be borrowed but
lent to end, surd swamped in dissent and crowing in the ignorant Labor
victory, Tory surprise, smaller sun not even gabled to the humping
whig, duty of a telegraph, lits bet on eagerness and Alexander's night
like club, like a cartouche lancing the Nile of its previous oracle
nightly understood eventual tissue, barbed bonnet, nubby mons, roll
taker, LITTLE biggest other, enormous cleopatriated yesum begat
on the bugatti of my best seat of MARS y PAN, ancestral doomsday cowardess
of treacle, origin of oxygen and this lesson, old enough to know
better young enough to care, age 1999, lit on sleeping legions plastic
sutured debris of my prairie, words for the ballerina of KEYNES' eye
Chris sent packing to the cellar rose of outasight, correct as Tess

itura, librarie of the staircase, mirageous tome, empty niche
this latch, home away from home, birthday-suit day is PREGNANT
'always been, since regents preferred backyard beer, word data
longing for a heart in space, anti parse, any heart of yours
will do, these times are ours, sibylline palatino, bodoni, gill
bride of BEMBO and petite fille of my granjon, minion dense
to futura, apple of my type and soul of all my mortal jumpstart
reciting Vespers, carmelite Genoa, snow candy, triple twinings last
dawning, glove daddy, galvanized and lemonsent bucket of
wet lowdown, quick duck, quiet storyteller, thickest set adobe, deed
er and dumbo, tent ears couped incapable of CLOSING, famous
old French equivalent, GARE monde, Arles let et penned-in vichy
eau, who died the same day she did, sauce, piff, dead like a Parisian spar
row dyed in cock tow, crowned where it's FORBIDDEN not prohibited

to walk upon the grass, more duty than privilege, given skirts
enveloping panda and the pang of my Chinese booker's wear, e'er
spending makes it so, so homosexual English marriage mistakes
the AUDITION, or does he leave its tanner noticement of vulgarities ammo
rican, to win or lose, nothing, Schwinn Raleigh of your foot pedal
down Fiona's darkened way, your west road backside up on
my easter, Persian piano, born to its mirror, more Empsonic
than Leavisite, faster than a SURVIVORS photograph, more sweet
than dawn, hesitant elision, birth of my arembour thus thrown in Seine
like guts of belief binned for engines of love, tender reluctance, kissy
stroll, gamble to GRANTCHESTER, mill bust, closed at bridge close
clowning twentieth of nove mar, smiling out of night and day smiling
hunt and dent, suggested, proposed, prescribed, and facing the edifice
to be lit guest, love forth with a life don't matter, mon oiseau, be it so

faucheux de mon île, germaine who makes me pause for gee
se, Brits fed for homeless journalists, Ian's Norfolk auntie, unkosh
er squid at PEPYS'S lackluster nose, snoozing queen's
attorney, curly cue, fried lander, benstocking banger
of redundancy, saffron walled in, test true ants, Count No's birthday
night out on paint, great awakening awoke to WAKE, finickie lain
heath coat walking to the clamor and exploding fireflies ere
some other gesture of anti-semite dose-reading, smallish
sandy-scripted seemstress, Arabella enforced cave of suspiciously nice
Petrans, Indian confidant devoted scout, unsuitable unsie
sable salmon, poetic altar made greater by the PILL and the able question alter
nation, sleeping with the only way to speed up DAY'S other wedding
my nostalgic dudess on the backs of porpoises, heaving to nemesis, numb
Isis fishing for really big carp with week-old cupcakes, crummy

apologies for breasts, saint of the altercation, first tea
cher, seconding poet, AND I liked the poultry, and the reception
history with a glass of iced port like Keats, candle lighter
by the toilet of gestureless gauds newborn, weather flown
to me through the chunnel straight from raw penthouse archer
strung loading, misdirecting and forgiven VERGIL, crossed
Lethe, Helen's sisterly scolding at the eavesdropped landing
doc banked by the iffy other, amazon truc cantaxable nexus
subjunctive of grammar, indirection of my objective, mistaken
dative fire of LAMBSKIN, joy of my life on lamb, like light
not born yesterday but here for a moon, born again when eyes
resisted to be laid on butterfly stomachers, CLOWNS
middrift riding to Camberwell Station, dump, enduring nag
ging ginseng, cough, trot, cumberbund and bath, crooked be gin

unmelting cantor, unmentionable tie, Peterborough's yellowian striped
chemise, free woman do as you please, SKI jumping jet adore
ajar agape, villainie jargon and indecipherable blab, second first
accuser with a sigh or PINKIE wobbling, not my matter, for little matt
er's love, adornment of Pippa's passing, Kings, your Queens and our Jacks
and ten thousand senile whispers at the Spade and Beckett, not a U, sect
aryan club, SCR, plodge, hall, and the reflectory, poor Ryan's
minute second and still third of horologic time emit, slot or no
mad life, endgame, check mate, range clock, my leaving, rubber
nubbin shedding orange crumbs across the rubbed-out équipage
era sure of something while it lasted, first for a second, two, one
betimes, some peristalsis of a Browning poem, LIBIDO leaves the world
for word of my world, world of your word, ugh, my chuff, my flitch
the repaire of Bacchus, juice consigned to daraf or farad

wins or lings, mattressing firescape, closet girdle close it
corsair, moon over their backs, our unholy Chinese scholar of eight
eenth century études, wool stone-crafted of my Christminster
student at glassy store window, fortunate for next day's breeze in
terior, ciel interior clamps it fine, hopeless tome lying windless in display
redder flaneur of my passing along it, RUE, peering fenestrienne
at my sill, my ledge, here's some for you, love of some life
or other, yours or ours, hear, theirs were you, and there I was
yours, ugly gaper taken for a scout, INK froze at the cobweb,
glass reflection carried to the French, the Egyptian, ajar Tennessee
walkers, door memory, little my bean, SHAG rug of the absent
script, posted banns, my letter's bin, even after nevermore again
our noon, dear for bears, still listening periplump, forbear of pallid DIS
cryption, Peter porter, my lees, inverse reporter, do re mi for Jesus' sake

forbear recording my style, type, pet, gear, ring, poult
ice, waste of woman's fascicles, my career, robber KIT, waistrel
of my envelope and discrimination, invisible blacklisted
envy of elopement, yank discerning corn, Marlborough's
death in Queens, blindered foal of the Nineties folderol
all over, scaffolding of fustian delivery next door, mon pi
erre, mon olivier, plin LEMONY chronometric of sorts, plea
sure of the quotidian pain threshold now quite auto gar
aged above the abandoned bakery in FELTON street, number one
squat from Stanford, middle OUP of my Jamesian period, crib cabin
style three thousand years on from your Trojan filly, lux
or my late placent, divine but not yet marred by Gibbsy imaging, son
net of Venus and MARS barred by synchromesh, ash folie, mine haha
Elizabathos of one poem not forgot, jetted lady not quite blank

but blue lit out of John Smith's tube, it should have been out
of question, out of sync, out of mind, out of sight, out of tissue
and coming from that place called Beyond Belief, outta fags
cut to CLOUD setting, Boodles, St Antony and Juliet asleep warm don
key bier instead of debt, books and pose's future lost to the Lady
at Norwich, stolen by the Pittsburgh steeler like the image
at Ste Elizabeth's, new directions' cloudy drawstring indeed, tick
borne at the babolie tour, hunger woman, fire cracked lover, infant regard
er os, adorning pips and kings, cut to my arm forever like a tree
limberer than FACE to truth's face, words which become a mouth
whittled in flight for all seasonable remains, reaper, whip, seminarian
mumbling operas everyday, melancholic tucks, virgins scuttling
fictive seaclaw, mouth open for fountain milk, phantom remains Jung
frau version to my RALEIGH, his snakebite at the Champion

of the Thames, c'est moitié, next door to this bastard birth
day or beneath it like a congealed block of lead, left there
for performance value in the mud, or are we talking dredge
here, sweet SOFT runner, hallmark, melting lamps, bencher can
not of my look at you, suckled ticket, my keep unkempt
comer to Jesus upper hall, shy CURRYMATE, immersed droopy e
yes, foot times ten times fourteen and doubled endlessly, visit
or unlamped, discrete and obdurate open-ended egg, key
holed bedder, brooding bleeder, flutteriest nest, sky
of grazing, sky of night, my lady geyser gazing wader into
dowaging FENS, fluid jump in Cam after first jump er
mine immersion, my aftermath, after talk, after honeyed
whispers, tailored limbs, reticence, after camp, after work, Rod's 6000
after love, after lunch, after job, something else, afternoon chair, sleep

and night after night after night after night 'til night's knight
ed, post-dated ergo proctor hocked, post ed, post it, post CHECK, post
humous and spread ayes around by BEDDERS, first sect of the club, post
erior to the lost girl's posture upon entering the room, chamber
share's postulate, roast and cheeks so pillowed on the week-old di
van, quite nice, Fragonard de Bougereau, EOSOROEO in honey jar, aux
ours, tumble in a cup of Christate welcome and some protestation of cha
ins noise after midnight, that complaint of Mr Kiss, the grey gay scarf of
President Histoire de la Raj, empirical need for brown-skinned lovers doubt
y miss, my scream, my palms to cheek, FINGERS, lips, leggy e
legy, fiddling willy-roaming burner of my boiler plate, bunted stint
ed good wife, reticence after residence, rusty iron employment, E
mall, red road, sub-atomic bet future like the monarch flies, inter
not, Kings of gin, O leave me no doubt, giddiest revival of atom

ic events, dead aim, hot rock, how miss, aimée, little mag
got brain, tangy will for hoarfrost, want for silence, O lip syn
ching stairway to heaving, NADIR V, kitchen itching I
Ching of toiletries, leaping buoy, Yerba Buena, my destruct
IVed doughboy in some fabulous reproximation of ma
tron not any el man at kin germain bier could prick there
you'd think, TOOT suite, these few decades of gender now will co
arse agander, good God at the end of the ell ipsis no less, love's ex
cuse, cascadent nincompoops, sift greater than policies, pal
ace of the seat of marsy panopticon, hilt of my noose, sea rebel
lion, robinesque think-tank, hawker of foreigner poe
tries, largesse for eigner, window comrade, SNOOD of woman like
a man snoozing, landing life east of fastening, feast of friend
ship, willies upon our meeting maw, Bernhardt ear

rings faux natal day delivered, prevaricating gardens knowing
full well harnessed to true thought, HACKAMORE, khakis, pen
insular daughter, circumscribed text, uncircumcised bit un a
wake like you like me like hymns, indulgent sheet, one dog Gar
y's snog-hope, grove, threads, pillow next to my pills, sleeping
kids, aides, my governess, the good much harm does thee, nuts
and locks and the FASCICLES' hysterical manner of apocalyptic
drawers, elle not mine but still meant to be HERE, show above
the wash, DELPHINIUM overarching blue lobe fatigue, coin in poc
ket, Keats' billiard ball and evening's morning starred, mon
ie last card ensconced in leather, anathematic sorry apothegm, anchored
brow, academia, soothsayer, oh Klingon, good for series or ambered
harems of THOUGHT, logorhythmic shift, swaying madam, noon's meridian
donned survivors, dawned upon ideas acamp the dawn, gills' forfeiture

my lady's lastima, fleur du val, chinese mulatto, shawl
of the shoulder of my epaulette, examineuse, sutped
mouth, DOOFUS, my knot caught in unexamined termination, bur
sar's file, Rymers IBM check, checkers, human being, love's labor
last Coleridge said or meant or smoked, dose at midnight
wife, kid, no matter the cradle, palestinian address, sun
pointed punctuation of EDIT my ED said, it's tamer red let
ters simply mistook, liège, school's ledger, already you
rs before mine, before me like a reader, tits, a cloud theory of
repetition's advance, hours not ours before us, too y
ours like doors, and every day was done to me like a poppy to its
sun, eyes, mouth, and nose—and here you sent the little petrie dish
continuous HAPPENSTANCE, posted hours, dumb white cheese
in throat, the grimace of the painted face making war with mirrors

scrims, rimshaw cosmetics, bargains in red leather at marketplace
the reassuring obscenity of this proscenium, decoy, mine armour
indian inherited tendency of the Catholic, TLS commons tarries
souls wronged by whom, so little fidget, loss to words, may
hem, INITIAL eaten, release my verb, my void, my gulf, my word
red sea, middle earth, Caribbean, thumbs tax, descend
ant, push-pinned chamber, everywhere it's written, cant
arabian unreconstructed glove, my GLOBE, rump rotund torrid
in the sunny dirt, above and that below, Ste Elizabeth's kanga
roo courtship, amour caned with a whip, lashed to mastheads
mustered by SIRENS canned not heard, ice in Newfoundland, miss Lovey
kerosene heedless of engines, ash without fuel, freezing BODICE, tank
topped libertine, draculatrice of my neck of the woods, Vlad
amor Boadicea, Scarus, my source, eros, ma punaise, philopornic Keynes

EGYPTE my philippine, antsy Egypt's Egypt, pelican flagon of the
dragon USE to be, unspent youth at Rossall, my Peloponnisse, hi-
de-ho, queer young love, my embarrassing constructed Muscovite
rain, cagey be pinned, mirage of rummage, interrupted reign
picture show, Stonehenge papparazi, Mandy Rice-Davies of the right
whiggy left, Lady Douglas, TIGGY boff copping the nod
of HARS, illiterate legitimate chalice from the palace, my T
rue brew, instructress in the art of eating tresses, CB 1 hands
maintenant, cold, incapable and fired past cut, little tit
mouse in the watery vase of ENGELSLAND, my work, gym excuse
so then however, still rune, running my room, your own blood works
Mexican periods, chink wall, pub wife, rude adieu, row with you, mon s
eduction, stupefying dues, my leave, my escape, sue, just an es
capade anesthetized truth, that lay in lying true, route tereu and men

ace deuce, W doubles you, wet groom, will you, wall of my willow, mar
rye me, cambrioleuse intent, veil and scrim, hearteastart, arabes
que of Nicolas Poussin, Jerusalem of me sachem, cunnilingual of lang
spiel syne, cheap necklace priceless, dear ignorant sanscript critique
camel drive, broker's straw, light of my HUMSPENT loins, cantaxi, major
ette of lamps at liger, march abril in her undiscovered land
scape, return, my returning mood, américain musician, reeds
shorish MORSEL, ma pétaudière, cold trifle left upon fed peter's
luncheon, huguenot hung with laurels and proud flesh, unreturnable mars
hall of my prefecture with a scar for PIPPA, tartuffe et flitch
organdy of this testament, bay, swatch and cotillion of inter
missions, window of mares and main of the windup of MANES, forgiven
ess of sea and of grants, here and there till end time, specialest
diadem inherited unbeknownst, ephemurgent occasion gone, gain

sway professor, postultimate young recruit ready for land on vir
gin or Coventry, posh nutter (SNOG), daft laurel Byzantine swimmerette
allegoric search for vitamin Z, reach for chum, little shark's sleepy
inhalation of watery buckets, ephebian snowdream, texte germain, soda
fountain where Dr Johnson took caffeine, mysogene of St James
snowball, Queen's chance in the maw of Ruggieri, regal sneeze
of Elba, father's presence for me, my preference to lie with an
other, Helen unabducted from the island, absent brother, horsewhipped
lover orchestrated for audition of MAY'S anthology, rich crusade first
returned verbeaten, mother, waylaid in France, sprecht nichts der Englisch
per functionary poésie, if not down then richly dark, float and jet ad sum
Samson's testimental agony with pillars, mere fascicles hanging fire
in the overlook courtship, mature, GREASED and victorious, like war
bler at castle wall, somewhere Chaucerian like the grave for norm

and Di, enthroned a whistling caballine, my casement, sarsaparilla
mild sélavy arises a rose, camellian palaver, mouse and apple of my Mercedes
miles from thee DOXIE swallow, palindramaderry of palestinian French, net
thrown for the Sun photographer, my pause, Welsh tampon di
ed reading tabloids, W. C. WALKMAN buttoned into OFF, graft of Fa
ti ma in funky green Medina, luci melos, don wan dawn redressed, par
ties pelmet both coming in and going out, ears on whopping pillow
chronicles shot with shutters, such exposure welcomed coming aye
yes aye on the prod unit, syrup at sunup, cough drop at sundown, exa
mined plunge into immersion, beddy TEDDY Davidian of the scrum
halved behind dears, children, Waco wrong before Avery's woeful element, tears
dearth, I'm dead, you're not, we know, THEy're dead, eaters in theater, pals
bosoms, some one frank gift who gives a damn, Janites co-opted sonitu
suopta, pall bearing SOUVENIR of re-venue, seized delicto TRUCK in car

Nadine, DIN of my wish, English winner of Johns against el ton
of postmodern fisheries, recycling station buss in eternity's embrace
dumb sing of my shinola, amazing what mothers can do once they put
their KNIVES to it, mon surprince, what the fuck, countess, indiscrete kiss
er, telling fuckEE from fuckER, out of lantana, materialist ex
mate, excuse my language, 'sbedder driving, morning sublime, moaning, pre
judice like another, the preferences, the abstinence, the sectarian
institution, lioness of self control, frog of sexual excess, candle of a woman
you know you know you know you know my source, au jus, secret
est position, ineluctable model, filmy star, flimsy mate judgment in
visible, Keats's error, post-Bengalian tide, used to be, mine ire
ne goodnight, pull it on in and let me check yr oil, goil, my tank
or yours, o'er TOP my pit, subsequent cabriolet and fadedness
of lets, tabula rastaferrari, starfuchsia heliocoptered to desert agin

court initial on your lapel, my 'scool Adam and St John, insect repel
lent to the skinny legions, back and side go bare beside, drinking
lambkin still meets my eats, sleepy breast, hollow phobafranc, hung
er of my neck, Engelsland LASSO, apology for living long, all along
the theater, desire for breath, braintree, love of cold flesh, blair
morite green, groundless and sanidine, your dead stick outside my window
all ready flush and pecked, living hand to France maintenant, wet wits whim
sea view, children play pleasure, my MESS, a muse and thatch
er on backing breast, scared crow, sacré coeur, pleasing some mort
onic gods or OTHER, being amongst them, your name in its subject,
III Elizabeth ans, sorrier elle, je t'aime natal cracks, national character, rachet
keyboarding type, acting, making, sorrow insular, soeur et ma
juscule, totalless sum in me in you and you 'n' me, where's yours, my tendon
memory Biblical, sweet watered burning BUSH of my testament and the testi

monies meant oriflamme, bitch of dogmouth, sod revetted lit
ter of my consent, geeze louise sartorial sartrelessness, liv
ing breath asleep in your KOFI, my warmest cape, vint
age John, beau voir, my ballerine, ammo, some exit
a moss a MATER, anon Matherite, my preternatural te
at my shiite, Mossad, once my clitheria of boul EZ
blue worker at dumb place, dauphine, docker, scavenger ben
gerite, pocket for your hand, CAJOLER, cringe reader, read
ing gaol, at Tica and eagerest angel, fiendish turn at fir
ing night's movie that sleeps still in slow motion, Wilde's sent
essence, erect SEER, eerie question, Auden to Larkin, end of Engels
landish poetry, forgiveness forgetting, governess of unpredictable child
run of future, the future of memory, matrix of the METRO
polis, eyes upon a rock, my head of stone, for an hundred years, e

coli like tickets baby, rest, truss, the rest of me, moitie of me T
rails, courageous trial, my newt of GEESE, my love of posies
petunias, my favorite American flower and poultry of brain
ard, sweet pea of my pop one happy hour, can of bourne
mouth, knownie knowns, whiplash, my back, past
oral of senior tutorial, muddied refuse, projective pet
er out NOW, mon excusez-moi, grandness, rhapsody, ma direct
rice jack hues, look after you, look on, one, only aft
er my duty collapsed, elapsed unseeded LAPLANDER, alas at
last for that, LOOK for you, afterwards, after math, after long, A
ward, de guy at the golden section of de board with
name for it lasting at last, 'Swanker along the water fronting on
back of Magdalene, adventuress HALF, sung at lea
st my way, my eye, yard, deed, it's dictaphonic no more

no—more sleep walking back to be back again, em pres
sure against the backs, QUOTES front door at the tit
le page, sweatered thief, extreme pretending to try
out for Beatrice, out for blood, for love or money
out of loneliness in a crowd of consorts pale as all
get-out, get-up from Cancer Research or from Crips
greatest corner of the market maunday wed
nec pas, sweet Thames in Seine by southside of Arno, R in S
treet outside of church, INDISCRETE policy, so thinking
makes my gulf, my GIBBETINE, my else, made so, my dolt
ie digit, turgid eddy, nattes s'il vous plaît, nothing is but
thinking so, want of place, our place in end, my rights are
mine or yours, OURS, cursed NEED for company, go seedy scram
bled eggs, broken shell, stolen letter, my scam, my bo

ok leaping bear, cake, choice, right to left of
life, leaving one born two, the spring, first green then Dis
appearing back at white whey, please, leaving women's lib
ido arriving station stoked on KENT, lent to lash
me to mast, after silent Brahmsian concert O Syl
vie across from the ballerina of the Kings' master,
lateliness sprung up in Armenia, Arizona's sweet djersy
ma man, word, warden, world, sentence, light, weird com
MISSION, one on one, responsible, unspoken, untalked to invincent
gêné, grass, John nudged, not minot, me and rue, moët et moi, el
bow's daughter, law your letters kill, my STILL illegal ability
to respond, sister Jude, panhellenic Nell, receiver of overlook
last word a woman says, bridey headress in local folderol, di
spenser of love with night pricking on Harrods plan

for mummy, pop, juice, AEGIS, et my quailling eggs at some bo
som of the other, dodgey slant six, hedgey southern pig
scrotum, thoughtful grease, love of space, sun, dice
y feat, air, fire, and the soiled element, o'er my hesitance to read
your word, material matter, man hat mad gone fall ope ra
yon ersatz futures sold, ORANGINA, prone to gigantic clemen
tines, short of diesel, maybe June, Jane, Nick, John, Nell, hairy
millenary, son petitioned James, spirit for the dark, S. J., tor
rent shall reign, no apology, my thatever neverminded, bon sang beau
clerc, templed weakness, wishfulness, bucolic truth, levitation of philo
SOPHIST chemistry, Lavinia, fissure, all sisters of Levin
ass, favorite lecturer after me, red knot, ampersand, levia
thon, unread book, caesurae, kind of gynecology, bottle of STEVE
NOT, bollocks blood of EGER antsy for the dansant and its tent amount

to some kids, wont, must, will, memory, summa
wrestling with the idea that a word is the last thing
any woman will say, this will will say, your old wish W
as my command on THOMPSON'S LANE, commatossed retirement to
the thirteenth of your retirement, O endless and tireless desire
for oft-flipping mantle, kea n'est pas, vespers, ne me quitte pas
angie DICKINSON on the rear seat of the VESPA pulling
wheelie in the middle of Genoa at five in the afternoon, O
ur snug rug movie in the afterglow off Leicester Square's double
life and sun, remembering reader, eventually burnt for Lorca dung
est putred flesh at last, put right, done WRONG, puttering
out neighborhood destiny, irretrievable chet-whinnying Kos
ovo, nest of vipers, LAP of plays, curds and way, whole corn, then my ser
pentecostal WITNESS say Jeremiah, voluptuary bar and goal

darned in red dressed imagination, alway ironic survey
of three a.m., matter before class, droll redress, exacting fat
ter insisting before lunch, failing of rolling, ad sum,
emerald throne of Kings, seat of Mars, the rôle, misjudgement
interest in the list of gifts, journalist from ELLE, miscalculant
masculinist PC critique, debt and whirling spindrift, hoar
frost, dish, my YVER wish, fulness, wrong, uprightliness, that bitt
er bridge, drawers thrown in Seine, doff celantro phenom da
shed upon a sliver, back to the future Benjamin, false spring
wedded assist, anti mon O tone, c'est moi, pas un moineau, Henri
ette wooing cross the CHANNEL, lame vein, my sol la
me, noh-brainer, tissu en lamé, wooden bridge, London
lecturer my louvre, disposition there to LOVE, instead of lou
er, rue et rivière, applest indulgence, VER, boarded key, silly fan

tasty of our overemphasis on reading, while our hearts
gasp dying for want of leave, buttress in place of which WH
ere we took whop, poultriester why not come my P
lump, latest pregnancy on couch of first coming the
re, bound Magdalene after FULL moon, ED's aborted tale of Tunis
mail my date, fig, basket, fountain, pen, birthday sting, erupt
ion echo deafness of twosome, late Latin rain at Mill Bridge
where first you swept me o'er, natalic day, my eyes
your lips, our nose, your EARS, later mouth, resistance, D
own with LUCY, thatch, bra, what's-her-name, cake, natch, o'er sut
ure, ditch and our indulgencies, round big paper glo
be, O smile at last to leap in Cam, glamour murdered lieb, Hud
ders fief, glandsome sleep, re joice and my fey, toilet down
habitual seat, uplifterer MS pissed down under LEAVES tabled

for humped camel at O a SIS, oat culture, question
what does England matter on the sandy linen sack and
mattress of the new, MIRANDA without banns, backs, lowdown
new African world, bebop formalism, lost body in the three
foot mogul outside Algeciras, AU bad date with Bowl
es, Wilde sentence, Auden to NYC, A.G. feed, burning mattress doux et
sweet the ford-bought vulvas, everyday disappearance, drink at the
backs, recruitment into REAL scholarship, some salman-crowded eve
ning, ma damn seniority, inevitable minority, señora, sinus, be
gin drinker, butler, be germinant, evenings, stoned MUD, petering
out the bollocks day, ming dynasty, instead Hampstead
darling south of mapstead Heath, love of life, balm
y spar, SPARE country pied 'sblood, buffy jockey puffy boxer, barbar
ian's flag, mon fritchie do, nurse, guide, done guard, har

binger of bang and bantu, scarlet dunghill of SMOKE, after orators ma
boule of goldfoil, arabic necklace, chumps change monarchie, my beat Y
our mom, you bet your ass, asthma butt, little girl grownup ta
bou teen train to Sister Nasser's sea at last, writing person, wild rustic
ation to rue St Jacques, official parsonage, flame of my ORIFLAMME
and there goes English Poetry for fifty years, Briggflatts
day of days, longest suture, tea, next-door virginity and gigantickest co
ach, TEACHERS pick-changed breasts, tradition, waitress iron married flam
marion, slantwise creature of grand parents, coquetterie at why not the
sinkola, Di's DNA mummied to her will, cleaning up and out, MI-5 break up
start unknown dirt, rim of the job, QUEEN E's instruction, black list of join
ers, Jimmy's cues, Eddie's BANK, tunnel photos, wet rain blowing more
faster than the small rain down can reign, song, substantiation, secret
ion in a cell of perpetuity, pussy at the college evensong, mulch et amore

Apollo Feast at Peterhouse Sir Gilbert, dim sung obsession of Emerson
ian surprise, Deutschland wreck, Hopkins' budgerigar, Twiggy boost
tidal lid the glance of sleepers, crunch of hopes, moment's ink
ling in my room, prefect CHANGE of your c(h)amber, sir
een ladder of extinguishment, well, Pater's tale, mattressed in a hairless
bowl of stories, creaming mentor of cheery dementia, sis
ses' jacket little mole, disguised MINION, S & M girl, car lien
dancing in photographs, gloves, gown, grown-up ex
tension of torn bathrobe, rye, crumb, load, wcw.com
plexion tied to burning blush, Daddy's SCOTCH, cherries, mother's par
king lot, MY mother's sleeping in her nappy-damasked chair, the
message that she glides, she slides, she glides, her
asking for HER mother, their speaking for derided US, try
ing to get them eat soup, plaque, tangles, hair, phoneme sex

tant amount to rest, careen off career, applicant, gent
lest dismissal of resilient love, I am the ONE who
's leaving, decided deciduousness, laddie of my fire
extinguisher, Papa's absent ROPE ladder, sent, mot
hers husband, juste, will a catheter, sound shakesperience God
did well with me, whose rooms like Maudie's looked on Cam, old
use to my married Christ, like Mrs. Aldingham, slight, tender
and white, less lesbian born, briar, scam, amazing one, little
completion, you baboon, tumescent LIZARD, waisted ro
se, mine eros, mine armour, negro: cheap fifth
of Bull's Blood aus Hungary, né Nicholas regret, inlet
Sausalito, EGRET winged with oil, next Warwick
stories from couch stand, sandwich to leeward like OTHER miles
Cunitch of Halvard, Tale, Camford, Dex, Rum & Little

Dicker, you betcha Ellefont Castle, deux et dieux
tide of my JOINT and dealt of heaven, no idea what
made us or what MISSED and what passed, POCK et ASS
ass in NUMBER, possession, hall above and heaven belief
sister's rest, sham waste, your whisper, socks held by ma
tronage, can yon ardent fanny canoe reamed of MS Mis
sing from manuscripts AE nyad of sheepy hilloe, whoa, castle hill
site which came en temps, divan after and before war a dream
of yours, tine's wrath, little troth, murk 'n' mind act
ion you love over the top, over matchschtick, o
vary the norm over the TRANSOM, over the brink, over T, overt
rain, portal, lichen, overhung with drape and the dressing go
sling, falling apart on grass BED, apart from me, ap
art from you, apart from the story about some nick
ers apart from loins, about THEM from other body par

TS like a brain, an arm-heart, a bowel, a limb, around a pout, champ
pain shoulder, will or bur, i.e. lust to stay the inability to go aft
on braes, as men to unputoutable fires bubbling put out to past
ure marry the actress come upon by accident, skills for the imp
lausable trade of DRESS, for inertia, rippling red and white awning, comp
any gaze for your eyes, fortune for a WHISPER, all wet all right
loincloth for hook, big bath for New Year's cat, donkey, chicken, Keaton
with three or four barks, years, weeks, wanker, pant, board's week
ended US, indifferent to spoons, Basra-stricken, Bologna, veronica on silence
and silk, MAGDALENE pet, graveyard snog like some ability to move WH
ile lying still, chipping statue at back's sensation, back gar
den less than life-size and life-like, coming to, you're LICKED and left
running when running came, and my leaving running left recalled
put out deluxe and then put out delight before left leaves

e're leaving left, ghost snogging readerless wacko, wank
er friend, wilder girl, wide boyfriendship so JACO
being, ardent and intransigent, finalist dawning bullock last
nicked in bud in bed in mind in place of the placebo, address radical
& passionate, the REAL republic, no corny platonic alienating comeuppance
eremite riding on an elephant, the NEW projective SHAG RUG with mess
ages reigning dawn, Lynnie's blues bath at gatehouse adornod
ding club, dessertion of my dissertation, PRESENT 'til end of Lime Rickey
gives dark appearance for Coronation, o'ER wishes to be, forced
to be teddy, sequestered quarters, resignation, dis
appearances of the consorts of Kings, Gibbs good fea
ST, my NICK and my nor A, little yapping, Aster, re
marriage PROOF of the film with James Stewart, lunch
with Kelly, what acknowledgement gives, my grateful Dis

interest at the parade lane, blank film of your
happiness, countess too much, COUNT extreme, ser
ene silence of unspeakable delay, unfucking leave
ably beautiful waiter, tress, lateness to be slower to
church than hill, TICKETS in the MAG garden, dye
d in wool, borne in rain, lying still, stephan
otical last lay, current weakness for the Elizabethan
ate TRADE to become tiniest lantana, mistakes bought
of presence, allegory of undercurrencies and the
nick of birth, more dearth of hours, next second, orchid
my life, my bloom, clear unseasonable INFANTA, salvaging dry
dock, mute trial, friendship wary of friendship, sun, la vie
WS on view, hat lying dormant at ball, my SON, mon dieu, youth
ful jollity, wild child, blind, come here, my duck, bet chance

black or blue, like your browning eyes, is a bell obscene
off-stage, my bell your bell, my body of work at your work
place, mon coeur, my belief the earth is sleeping
with the trees, some habit each night to pull the cover up
and chuck the chin at hem of moss and BARK, hand held main
tenant, taxi derm, to drowse nightlong in awe of cheek or storm
and marriage clang, scares me, uprightliness of mates, arise Laa Laa & Di
psy B'laire, yank nimbus watch pervades easterly as opportune as
music always had in mind canoodling the finale, finally her
aldic tift, Hellenic vendor, from the top pearl asea, spindrift
off marjoram, my dot, my mousse, mon blanc, mein Jung frau
FrouFrou CHOCoLATENESS both going in and coming out, whaup
whauven wheal, wengen and overland through dix fracas, craft, sink
soft and fidgety keyboard, sort, lieber freund, yesterdays spelt jeans

brook neige, nose for eyes, GIFT for torching Kettle's Yard, ich comme
accomplice, come, où s'éloigne what can who blindly spends, mob
ile posture, itching kitchen I Ching, juke box of your specialty, monk
et greyhound, my untied and my made knot, whiplash, mai
den all gone, nothing overdone, drinking lands more full
than enough, and my too much just enough, très sor
row Virago of this former BIKE, love, comrade, queen and middle
sense that sweetest scent, felt spinning ball John Keats sent
from handle of too early consumption, Sug Daddy thrown by many
generations of horses, all the music above accomplishment, garde ta foi
gras, shaving glass, can DUCK, liver watch, dew et
sons, yOU'Re on, femme, fain, ergo more sum, bit wee west of here there
what's-her-Caesarina, bridehead, identity the continual face
lift, ACCOMPLICE, wagging frozen tale, crying laughter, high thread

shot leaving now going PAST gone

ofT outside and in between

TWO

palimpsested a nimals tha

t repeat

themselves by RE

fusing to speak

A.. GAIN, R.. AIN B.. ORN, C.. OUGH

sky

RiVERBANK

libido leaves the world wool dyed

mons

trance

con fig

eru junk

defer

ance

well

-met coquin DOING

mon canard

Damned Car

Dammed Care

dranac nom

STEWED AND FRAUGHT WITH BIRDS

STEWED AND FRAUGHT WITH BIRDS

for PA

Oafs emit the fundament
                    on beaverboard
          flung to capsules
mistaken for supposition

The French like their medicine
                    up the wazoo
          as it gets to the livers
quicker than a speeding bullet

Of course DELEUZE
                    lept toward his lost breath
          counterfeit and discrete in
his choice of suicide by ventilation

To-wards the courtyard like any other
                    thoughtful smoker
          more vague than tall buildings and taught
to be a vertical philosopher at last

Socket, sill, lunge and shutter
                    wrench the lobes
          scrutinized for links
to two of clock face in his case

Times change and lo, time changes
                    though a glass of wine
          looks the same, like Paris
where babies still are made to mold

We understand the autobus of alcohol
                    is dangerous
          a tobacco for saintliness
though consummate à la mode always

Some reason to write in order to read
                    smoking a Chesterfield
          for Queer theory
appointed to the emphysematic company at hand

Pregnancy's the only job worth having
                    when to be set free
          is the proverbial function of the truth
which leads quicker to death than nature

Descartes had it right
                    with his socks
          before those fires in the country
and the desire to think in writing

When some bar has heat we sit
                    vertical instrument whiskey
          which perched reasonably
we stay awhile

You have a better idea
                    write
          it down.
If not down get richly dark

The ligaments
                    of your phraseology
          will eventually get
put to some truth test or other

and you'll be lucky
if anyone reads
it with a big guffaw
or sneezes

My future daughter or son
could undergo
a bone marrow transplant before birth
even if he she has my profile or not

I guess we know
how wonderful
life can be
at the end of the 20th century

not far from l'Etoile
Invalides or the Champ de Mars
in a rent-controlled apartment without
a Dubuffet in the quinzième

Was it then you got up
on the wrong
side of the bed?
"Yes, I did. My side."

When some foam
be agogger
than other foam, go for it
depending on which side of the bed sits

well with you
rabbit warren
in an armchair
at the postmodern Detroit of choice

or FORCE:

what power suits
it, what chance
can still illuminate the happenstance

short of course of the de rigueur
sleeveless black
leather vest of academe
that reveals its brainy muscles at the conference

Ahem, when I hear the words
oh poésie
I reach for my pyjamas
and punch out the pillows in the living room

Comedy in France
is an honored
tradition
bereft of laughter

Caca boudin clinks
the intestinal skin
of its institution
then slides down the gullet on its own sleeve

to be noted later, still enamelled
at the back of sulfurous magazines
by some Beelzebub
looking for a contract on the Faust of the moment

For tons of recent clay
will cover o'er
this fatuous skirmish
in the next literary war

Bonne année anyway
                                to all troglodytes
                    now that anti-semitism
can be a racist analysis

and post-modernism net
                                and yahoo may become
                    social realism at last
as modernism was reactionary by definition

Readers will see
                                what I am
                    driving at
though I may not have a valid license

Our pockets need some rocks
                                will sink us sound
                    into the three-meter width
of the Ouse

Already there's not enough
                                and not enough is more
                    than enough and too much
is just enough already

I wouldn't mind a future
                                on another virago
                    or a Harley Sportster
to fly out upon

That's my plan
                                anyway, peuple roi
                    and you can sit still
on the buddy seat—I've got the extra helmet

If you put your arms
'round my waist
I will be
helpful to you when we arrive

Peel through the hot air belted
with the latest naked emperors.
Give the boys a sweater to match the girls
and undress the pretenders, to reveal the Dauphin

Even should we crash
at the plastic borne
and our rugsters still
prepare at school for *their* career

something will be ready and in store
at the princely corner.
Is free-falling truth the next beauty queen?
Whatever sets you free can snore for both of us

although the dumb, unidentified birds
I see are still
fraught and stewed
with feathers of identified *liberté.*

One thousand
& two hundred copies of
Mon Canard printed April 2000
at McNaughton & Gunn, Saline, Michigan,
fifteen of which are numbered
in Roman numerals I - XV,
and signed by
the poet

Stephen Rodefer is the author of *Four Lectures* and *VILLON by Jean Calais*, among many other books. He has taught at the University of Cambridge and at the University of California (San Diego and Berkeley), and now lives in Paris.